LIVING
AMONG
GIANTS

BOTANICAL TREASURES
OF A SEQUOIA GROVE

SHIRLEY SPENCER

Yosemite Conservancy
YOSEMITE NATIONAL PARK

YOSEMITE
CONSERVANCY.

yosemiteconservancy.org

Yosemite Conservancy inspires people to support projects and programs that preserve Yosemite and enrich the visitor experience.

Library of Congress Control Number: 2015918548

Cover art by Shirley Spencer

Cover design by Amanda Richmond
Interior design by Nancy Austin
Map on page 6 © iStock: FreeTransform

ISBN 978-1-930238-67-1

Printed in China by Toppan Leefung

1 2 3 4 5 6 – 21 20 19 18 17

For my best friend and dear husband,
Mark Gary Spencer. Thank you for many memorable
experiences exploring giant sequoia groves together.

Contents

• = giant sequoia populations today

Introduction

Giant sequoia trees are presently found in their native habitat only on the western slope of the Sierra Nevada mountains in California. However, the fossil record indicates that giant sequoias, their living relatives (coast redwoods and dawn redwoods), and numerous extinct relatives, once grew in a variety of locations in the northern hemisphere.

With their specific requirements of an abundance of water, plenty of open space, warm summers, and mild winters, giant sequoias share their forest space with many other spectacular botanical species. They are scattered, with their huge, arresting, russet brown trunks, among impressive stands of sugar pines, ponderosa pines, and white firs, along with diminutive species of graceful shrubs and stunning wildflowers.

Early botanists traveled to the Sierra Nevada to collect the seeds of giant sequoias to plant in botanical gardens, as well as backyard gardens, and on university campuses and large estates. Given that giant sequoias can live to be over three thousand years old, these specimens have not yet reached maturity in their new homes.

Due to their size, longevity, and grandeur, giant sequoias have the ability to inspire us and also challenge us to focus on protection of treasured places. Visiting a giant sequoia grove can bring perspective to our lives, fill us with awe, and allow us to dream. In every season, and even at different times of day, the giant sequoia groves reveal subtle nuances of character and life.

Enjoy a saunter amidst their antiquity and savor the beauty and quiet tranquility that exists in the soaring cathedrals of a giant sequoia grove. When you go, consider visiting these outstanding and accessible giant sequoia groves, most of which offer interpretive information in adjacent visitor centers:

- North Calaveras Grove in Calaveras Big Trees State Park
- Mariposa, Merced, and Tuolumne Groves in Yosemite National Park
- Big Stump, Redwood Mountain, and General Grant Groves in Kings Canyon National Park
- Giant Forest and Atwell Grove in Sequoia National Park
- Mountain Home Grove in Mountain Home State Forest

TREES

....

California Black Oak

California Hazel

Giant Sequoia

Incense Cedar

Mountain Dogwood

Ponderosa Pine

Sugar Pine

White Fir

California Black Oak
Quercus kelloggii

The deeply furrowed gray bark of the deciduous California black oak is host to scattered mosses and a variety of lichens. Large impressive branches soar skyward, tapering to crooked, thin, angular twigs. In winter, among the bare limbs, one may observe yellowish-green clumps of parasitic Pacific mistletoe, which can stress branches but also provides food and shelter for a range of birds.

In spring, the tender new leaves are tinged with pink and accompany dangling catkins. In summer, the large, green leaves have a generally oval shape and are deeply lobed, with the tips terminating in pointed bristles. In autumn, the large, oblong acorns are capped at the top with a small cup covered with fine scales, and the leaves turn a yellow-gold color, withering to brown. This oak offers a fine example of marcescent leaves, with some of the dead leaves remaining on the tree throughout the winter months.

The California black oak is a magnificent and dominant tree of the mixed woodland landscape but in sequoia groves will more likely be tall and slender. Acorns were a historically important food source for many indigenous people in California and are still utilized in traditional ways. A wide variety of wildlife species depend on the nutritious acorn to see them through the winter months.

BOTANICAL FAMILY: Fagaceae

ELEVATION: 650–7,900 ft (200–2,400 m)

DISTRIBUTION: Foothills, lower and upper montane

HEIGHT: Up to 115 ft (35 m)

FLOWER, FRUIT, OR CONE: A large, brown, oblong acorn (fruit) with a small, pointed tip

HABITAT: Valleys and slopes in mixed forests and woodlands

California Hazel

Corylus cornuta subsp. *californica*

Smooth, gray to light brown bark covers the many-branched trunks of the California hazel. It appears as a large shrub or small tree, usually spread out wide and sometimes forming thickets.

In late winter and early spring, the tips of many branches are covered with conspicuous, brown, pendant, staminate catkins subtended by swollen, green buds. In summer the large, bright green leaves are velvety to the touch. The female flowers are less conspicuous but if pollinated form an obvious fruit, wrapped green. As the fruit develops, it is a seed encased in a pubescent, green involucre. In autumn, as the leaves turn various shades of yellow, gold, or tan, the fruit matures into a brown, edible nut, similar to the cultivated filbert, enclosed in its wrapper, now dried and papery.

California hazel is found in riparian environments and moist or shady forests and woodlands. This denizen of the understory provides desirable, nutritious nuts for wildlife.

BOTANICAL FAMILY: Betulaceae
ELEVATION: 3,600–6,900 ft (1,100–2,100 m)
DISTRIBUTION: Lower and upper montane
HEIGHT: Up to 13 ft (4 m)
FLOWER, FRUIT, OR CONE: An edible nut (fruit) enclosed in a papery husk
HABITAT: Shady or forested areas, sometimes damp locations

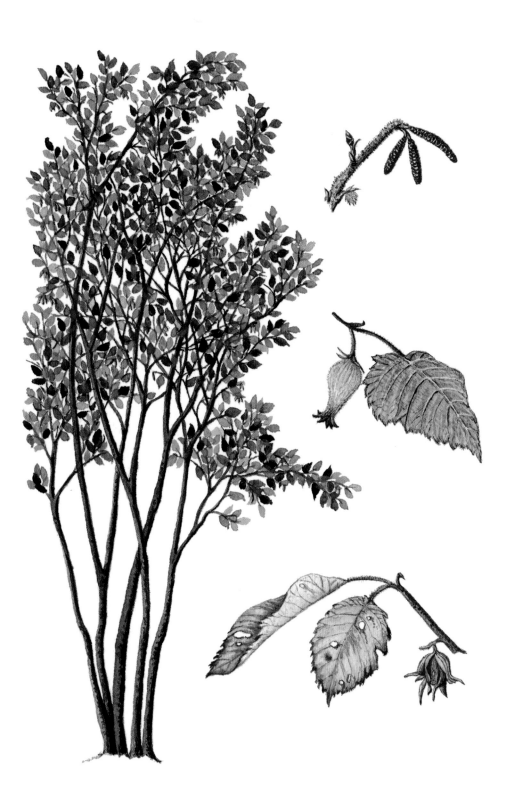

Giant Sequoia

Sequoiadendron giganteum

The mature trunk, which can be as much as 34 feet (10.5 m) in diameter, is sheathed in deeply furrowed, cinnamon-brown bark. The bark and foliage are similar to that of the incense cedar (see page 16), but the bark is spongy and fibrous, and the twigs are more three-dimensional, as opposed to flat. Near the base, the protective bark can be up to 20 inches (50 cm) thick. The large branches of the sequoia can have a diameter as great as the trunks of other forest trees. Small, bluish-green, overlapping, scaly needles are arranged along the stems in a pattern similar to the scales of a fish.

The inconspicuous reproductive structures can be difficult to see due to the lofty heights where they develop upon the tree. They can be inspected only when wind, snow, or a storm breaks off branches and twigs and they fall to the forest floor. Its green, egg-shaped cones can hang from the tree for up to twenty years, containing seeds that are mature and viable, but not released. When severed from their branch by wind or animals, or subjected to smoke and heat, they become brown and woody, and the scales, which are fused with the bracts, open to reveal many layers of tiny, flat, golden seeds. The seeds are approximately the size of an oat flake and have a pale olive-green line down the center of two golden, flat wings.

Giant sequoias thrive with ample moisture, space, and sunlight. Prescribed fire opens up the forest landscape, exposes mineral soil, releases nutrients, reduces competition, and allows many young sequoia saplings to grow into successful trees.

BOTANICAL FAMILY: Cupressaceae

ELEVATION: 2,700–8,900 ft (830–2,700 m)

DISTRIBUTION: Lower and upper montane, subalpine

HEIGHT: Up to 295 ft (90 m)

FLOWER, FRUIT, OR CONE: Oblong, egg-sized cones maturing from green to brown

HABITAT: Open or partly shady ridges and basins with adequate moisture

Incense Cedar
Calocedrus decurrens

The incense cedar has some of the characteristics of the giant sequoia tree (see page 14). Among new visitors to the Sierra Nevada, the two species can easily be confused with one another, but cedar bark is hard and woody and the twigs are distinctly flattened rather than three-dimensional. The mature incense cedar has thick, deeply furrowed, cinnamon-brown bark. Lower branches are splayed and descend, while the topmost branches are held upright.

The small, overlapping, scalelike leaves are yellowish-green and have a flattened, feathery appearance. Pollen cones are found on the very tips of the foliage and are light brown in color. The brown, woody, developed cones are pendulous and, as they open, exhibit three parts: two outer scales that flare, winglike, away from the central septum. Because of their unfamiliar shape, these winged cones may be generously scattered under an incense cedar and yet never be suspected as once belonging to the tree. Two asymmetrical wings attached to the seed aid in its dispersal by wind.

Incense cedar is an integral part of mixed coniferous forests in the Sierra Nevada. It enjoys sunny, open, or partially shaded slopes, ridges, and woodlands. Its russet-colored wood has a pleasant aroma, and the crushed foliage has a spicy, woodsy scent. Some indigenous peoples utilized the solid bark of the incense cedar as roofing material for their dwellings and most of us have used pencils made from this tree.

BOTANICAL FAMILY: Cupressaceae

ELEVATION: 1,100–8,200 ft (350–2,500 m)

DISTRIBUTION: Foothills, lower and upper montane, subalpine

HEIGHT: 66–226 ft (20–69 m)

FLOWER, FRUIT, OR CONE: Small, brown, oblong cone with septum dividing two scales

HABITAT: Open or partly shady mixed coniferous forests and woodlands

Mountain Dogwood
Cornus nuttallii

Mountain dogwood in bloom is one of the many understory trees that late-spring visitors to the Sierra Nevada are eager to see. The gray, mottled bark of the trunk gives way to pale ascending branches with a decidedly candelabra shape that is obvious in winter but obscured once the large, summer leaves emerge on this deciduous tree.

The bright green, elliptic leaves are distinctly veined and taper to a point. In autumn, the large leaves take on shades of apricot, red, pink, and amber. Showy, white bracts that subtend the flowers are petallike and may have a pink blush to them. The bracts are sometimes thought to be true petals. However, the petite, greenish-white flowers of the mountain dogwood are clustered in the center of the petallike bracts on a convex receptacle. Once pollinated, they form bright red, asymmetrical fruits, tipped by a tiny black point, congregated tightly in a small, rounded head.

Mountain dogwood grows in a range of environments from moist to dry and open to shady, typically in coniferous forests and woodlands. This tree, which is on the small side, makes for a breathtaking show when in bloom, and many avid photographers visit the Sierra Nevada during its peak blossoming time (around May) to capture unforgettable images. In late autumn, some bird species like robins, pileated woodpeckers, and varied thrushes relish its brilliant red fruit.

BOTANICAL FAMILY: Cornaceae
ELEVATION: 3,400-6,600 ft (1,050-2,000 m)
DISTRIBUTION: Lower and upper montane
HEIGHT: Up to 82 ft (25 m)
FLOWER, FRUIT, OR CONE: Showy, white bracts in late spring, and clusters of red drupes in autumn
HABITAT: Shady or partly shady coniferous forests and woodlands

Ponderosa Pine

Pinus ponderosa

The Ponderosa pine has a massive, golden-brown trunk when mature, often with a sweet scent similar to vanilla. The bark is scaly and brown when the tree is young, and ages into furrowed, platelike structures that closely resemble the pieces of a jigsaw puzzle. When the tree is subjected to natural or prescribed wildfire, it will have charred areas at the base and in the cracks of the trunk. The branches are ascending and widely spaced, with lower branches dead or dying in the shade of the upper branches. This attribute of having a clean trunk in old age is advantageous to many conifers, as it deters wildfire from using lower branches to ascend into the crown of the tree.

Its long, green needles are bundled in groups of three, with a persistent, papery sheath at the base. When dry, the oval, brown cone has flared scales tipped with projecting prickles and winged woody seeds that lie atop the scales.

Ponderosa pine is a dominant conifer in the mixed forest environment. Sometimes it can be found in vast stands on dry, open slopes, ridges, and basins.

A closely related tree, the Jeffrey pine, is sometimes mistaken for the ponderosa pine, and at sequoia grove elevations they may even cross-pollinate. The cone is the easiest way to discern the difference. The cone of the Jeffrey pine is much larger and its scale tips are tucked inward. The cone of the ponderosa pine is smaller and armored with outward-projecting prickles. The bark of both Jeffrey pine and ponderosa pine can have a sweet aroma, so a scent or lack thereof is not a definitive way to differentiate these related trees.

BOTANICAL FAMILY: Pinaceae
ELEVATION: 1,600–8,500 ft (500–2,600 m)
DISTRIBUTION: Foothills, lower and upper montane, subalpine
HEIGHT: Up to 223 ft (68 m)
FLOWER, FRUIT, OR CONE: Oval, brown, woody cones with prickly scale tips
HABITAT: Open or shady mixed forests and woodlands

Sugar Pine

Pinus lambertiana

This impressive and largest of pines in the Sierra Nevada, the sugar pine, boasts purplish-brown, furrowed bark arrayed with flaky, platelike ridges. If the forest has experienced a recent fire event, this resilient pine will show scorched areas on its base. Its mature upper branches extend nearly horizontally from the main bole. The deep green needles, which are arranged in sheathed bundles of five, are typically 2 to 4 inches (5 to 10 cm) long.

Mature cones of the sugar pine are the biggest of any cone in the world, measuring from 6 to 23 inches (15 to 58 cm), and producing them takes two years. Initially, the cones are green and the size of a finger. They droop at the tips of the branches, where they often coexist with larger green cones that contain seeds but remain closed, as well as brown cones that are yet older and have opened and dispersed their seeds. When fully mature, the cylindrical cone is a deep, yellowish brown with thin, smooth scale tips. Atop each scale lie two large, winged seeds. After the seeds disperse, the scales bear a permanent indentation and color impression of the seeds.

Sugar pine is a major component of mixed coniferous forests in the Sierra Nevada. Many species of wildlife relish the nutritious seeds. The Douglas squirrel, also known as the chickaree, can often be seen efficiently stripping the scales to access the seeds, leaving the bare center of the cones, resembling dry, brown corncobs, scattered on the forest floor. Please leave all sugar pine cones in the forest so the seeds may grow into new trees and feed wildlife. The naturalist John Muir declared the sugar pine to be the most graceful and noble of all pines.

BOTANICAL FAMILY: Pinaceae

ELEVATION: 2,500–10,500 ft (750–3,200 m)

DISTRIBUTION: Lower and upper montane, subalpine, alpine

HEIGHT: Up to 230 ft (70 m)

FLOWER, FRUIT, OR CONE: Pendulous cones, sometimes over 20 in (50 cm) long, on branch tips

HABITAT: Mixed coniferous forests

White Fir

Abies concolor

....

When a white fir is young, the trunk is pale gray and relatively smooth in texture. As the tree grows in height and age, the bark roughens and takes on a dark brownish-gray color. The bole of a large white fir is deeply furrowed and generally vertically striated. As the shaded lower branches die back with normal attrition, sometimes the location of the whorl of previous branches can still be identified.

Brightly colored lichens, usually a neon, yellowish-green color, encompass the tree horizontally where branches formerly existed. Typically, these conifer-loving lichens do not tolerate being buried in permanent winter snow. Thus, the approximate winter snow depth can be gauged based on the level where the lichen begins to grow. Lower branches exhibit flat needles, arranged feather-like along the twig, while on the upper branches they curve tightly upward in a U shape. The needles grow out from the stem with a slight twist at the base, and their tips are blunt and rounded.

In late spring, tiny, bright green reproductive catkins hang beneath the stems, lined up in rows. Mature brown cones are held upright along upper branches and seldom drop off whole; they disperse winged seeds as they gradually fall apart on their branches.

White fir is found as a dominant species in open to shady mixed coniferous forests. Based on palynology studies (the scientific study of pollen), this fir is presently more abundant and widespread than it historically was. Being shade tolerant and fire sensitive, white fir now thrives in dense stands in areas that have not recently experienced natural fire regime cycles.

BOTANICAL FAMILY: Pinaceae

ELEVATION: 3,000–10,200 ft (900–3,100 m)

DISTRIBUTION: Lower and upper montane, subalpine, alpine

HEIGHT: Up to 200 ft (61 m)

FLOWER, FRUIT, OR CONE: Brownish layered cone held upright on the topmost branches

HABITAT: Mixed coniferous forests

SHRUBS

Bush Chinquapin

California Azalea

Greenleaf Manzanita

Littleleaf Ceanothus

Mountain Misery

Mountain Pink Currant

Mountain Whitethorn

Sierran Gooseberry

Thimbleberry

Whiteleaf Manzanita

Bush Chinquapin

Chrysolepis sempervirens

Smooth, gray to brown branches of the bush chinquapin give way to green new growth on the outermost twigs. The underside of the leathery, elliptic to oblong leaves of this shrub exhibit a golden pubescence, especially on newer leaves near the ends of the stems. The leaf edges are slightly cupped, and the leaves are paler green beneath and a darker green on the upper surface.

Spikes of small, staminate and pistillate flowers are held aloft at the apex of stem ends. When pollinated, the flower develops into a prickly burr. Initially bright green, the burr becomes chestnut brown over the two years it takes to ripen. The armored, mature burr splits open to reveal a hard, brown nut within.

Bush chinquapin is found as a common understory shrub, in open or partially shady coniferous forests, often forming a waist- or shoulder-high thicket. It is not uncommon for people to think this thick-leaved evergreen shrub may be related to rhododendrons, as they have a similar appearance. But that is not the case. Bush chinquapin is a member of the same family as mighty oaks: Fagaceae.

BOTANICAL FAMILY: Fagaceae
ELEVATION: 2,300–10,800 ft (700–3,300 m)
DISTRIBUTION: Lower and upper montane, subalpine, alpine
HEIGHT: Up to 10 ft (3 m), but sometimes reaching 33 ft (10 m)
FLOWER, FRUIT, OR CONE: Brown burrs (fruit) protected by a prickly involucre
HABITAT: Open or partly shady mixed forested slopes and rocky ridges

California Azalea
Rhododendron occidentale

This deciduous shrub is a showy member of the genus *Rhododendron*. California azalea is multibranched, with ascending branches of older reddish-brown, woody stems topped with new, bright green growth. Elliptic to oval leaves, light green on top and paler beneath, grow alternately along the stems.

Its large blossoms grow in apical clusters of umbels or corymbs and may feel slightly sticky to the touch. Their fused or partially fused flower parts are generally found in groups of five: five sepals and five petals. The funnel-shaped blossoms are white, and their upper lobes are usually splotched or streaked with yellow. The margins of the petals are smooth, but often the edges are wavy or ruffled. The conspicuous, exserted stamens and pistil protrude beyond the petals. A capsule-shaped fruit develops from the superior ovary, and when brown and mature, it splits from tip to base, revealing many seeds.

California azalea can be found in riparian areas or near permanent seeps and springs, under a canopy of mixed coniferous or montane forest. This beautiful native shrub is beloved as a harbinger of summer in the Sierra Nevada, and the heady scent of its flowers can evoke pleasant memories of experiences in a favorite forest setting. Numerous species of the rhododendron family are cultivated and prized for their beauty and fragrance.

BOTANICAL FAMILY: Ericaceae

ELEVATION: 3,400–7,500 ft (1,050–2,300 m)

DISTRIBUTION: Lower and upper montane

HEIGHT: Up to 26 ft (8 m)

FLOWER, FRUIT, OR CONE: Clusters of showy, white, fragrant flowers with exserted stamens

HABITAT: Riparian areas, seeps, springs, or moist meadows and mixed forests

Greenleaf Manzanita
Arctostaphylos patula

Greenleaf manzanita has numerous trunks and branches that twist upward in an artistic manner. The thin, peeling, skinlike bark has a warm, reddish-brown hue and covers the living branches of this beautiful shrub. In older specimens, there may be partial or entire branches that have died and are pale gray in color and perhaps festooned with brightly colored lichens. The oval, leathery, green leaves are paler beneath and a bold green on the surface. Notice the darker green leaf color which distinguishes this species from the similar whiteleaf (see page 46).

The petite, hanging, pinkish-white flowers are urn shaped. If pollinated, they mature into small, round, reddish-brown fruits, which are an important food source for wildlife.

Greenleaf manzanita prefers open, sunny ridges, slopes, forests, and woodlands. There are many beautiful species of manzanita in California, and on hot summer days all have the ability to transpire through their paper-thin bark. In plants, transpiration is the passage of water vapor through a membrane or pore. The evaporative cooling of transpiration causes the branches to feel cool to the touch—cooler than the ambient temperature of the adjacent atmosphere.

BOTANICAL FAMILY: Ericaceae

ELEVATION: 2,500–11,000 ft (750–3,350 m)

DISTRIBUTION: Lower and upper montane, subalpine, alpine

HEIGHT: 3–10 ft (0.9–3 m)

FLOWER, FRUIT, OR CONE: Urn-shaped, pinkish-white flowers maturing to small, round fruits that look like little apples

HABITAT: Open, sunny mixed coniferous forests and woodlands

Littleleaf Ceanothus
Ceanothus parvifolius

With its open, arched form, sweeping branches, and showy, blue panicles, littleleaf ceanothus is an attractive sight in the understory of Sierra Nevada forests. The lower branches are mottled green or reddish and have alternate, deciduous, three-veined leaves in small groupings on the stems. Most of the leaf edges are entire and smooth, but some leaves may exhibit a small indentation at the tip.

Tiny, blue flowers cluster together in an elongated panicle that takes on shades of misty azure. The fruit develops in late summer and is a three-lobed capsule that is mostly green but can be tinged with purplish-red tones.

Littleleaf ceanothus is found in open or partially shady forests and woodlands. Though they might be only waist high, any of the several Ceanothus species found in sequoia groves can form vast, impenetrable thickets, especially after fires. There are many species of endemic ceanothus in California, and some are prized as native plantings in home gardens because of their faint, sweet fragrance, drought tolerance, and beautiful apical clusters of white, cream, purple, or light to deep blue flowers.

BOTANICAL FAMILY: Rhamnaceae

ELEVATION: 3,900–6,900 ft (1,200–2,100 m)

DISTRIBUTION: Lower and upper montane

HEIGHT: Up to 5 ft (1.5 m)

FLOWER, FRUIT, OR CONE: Panicles of small blue flowers at the apex of stems

HABITAT: Open or partly shady coniferous forests and disturbed soils

Mountain Misery

Chamaebatia foliolosa

This low, evergreen ground-cover shrub is sometimes seen in vast carpets beneath mixed forest canopies. If one brushes up against a mountain misery while hiking, its dark brown, hairy stems with their numerous glands can leave a sticky, aromatic residue on skin or clothing, and the glandular foliage can impart a strong scent as well. The dark green foliage appears feathery, with close inspection revealing that each leaf is divided pinnately three times—dissected once along the stem like a feather, with the resulting leaflets divided in the same way twice more.

The small flowers with numerous yellow stamens are beautiful in late spring and early summer when blooming en masse. They have white petals and green sepals in sets of five. The pale brown fruit is a dry, leathery achene.

Mountain misery is found on dry, sunny (or partially shaded) ridges and slopes. The glandular and resinous nature of mountain misery makes it an interesting and integral part of natural and prescribed fire regimes within the Sierra Nevada. This small ground cover is especially adaptable to wildfire and quickly sprouts from the roots in burned and charred landscapes, sending up vigorous, bright green, feathery foliage.

Although it is in the rose family, this shrub is often called "bear clover." Some visitors to the Sierra Nevada find the scent of mountain misery disagreeable, but many local people and returning pilgrims enjoy the aroma for its ability to evoke fond memories of a beloved locale.

BOTANICAL FAMILY: Rosaceae

ELEVATION: 2,000–7,200 ft (600–2,200 m)

DISTRIBUTION: Lower and upper montane

HEIGHT: 8–24 in (20–60 cm)

FLOWER, FRUIT, OR CONE: White flowers with numerous yellow stamens on sticky stems

HABITAT: Mixed coniferous forests and woodlands

Mountain Pink Currant

Ribes nevadense

Mountain pink currant, a deciduous shrub, has multiple dense, crossed, ascending branches. Its smooth, woody, perennial stems are pale grayish-brown, with new, vibrant, green growth unfurling atop older branches. The soft, light green leaves are shallowly lobed and mimic the shape and venation of a maple leaf, in miniature form. The upper leaf surface is a darker green than the underside, and the stems are slightly hairy. If bruised, the foliage emits a strong, bitter smell that some people may find unpleasant.

The small, layered flowers of the currant droop in grapelike clusters. The outer pinkish-green bracts and red to pink sepals are brightly colored and resemble petals, but the true petals are white, shorter, and enclosed, and subtended by the bracts and sepals. This native currant produces a small, round, green berry that ripens to a glaucous blackish-blue color. Unlike its cousin, the Sierran gooseberry, which has fruit with stout prickles, the berry of the mountain pink currant has barely discernible soft hairs and is devoid of thorns.

This shrub can be found either in dense thickets or fairly solitary. Its habitat is the margins of wet to moist, shady or partly shady coniferous forests and woodland. The mature fruit can be made into jam or jelly, and some species of this genus are cultivated for food or as ornamentals.

BOTANICAL FAMILY: Grossulariaceae

ELEVATION: 3,000–9,800 ft (900–3,000 m)

DISTRIBUTION: Lower and upper montane, subalpine

HEIGHT: Up to 7 ft (2 m)

FLOWER, FRUIT, OR CONE: Pink sepals with white petals tucked within the sepals

HABITAT: Riparian and moist areas in partly shady forests

Mountain Whitethorn
Ceanothus cordulatus

Mountain whitethorn is an evergreen shrub with many arched, ascending branches and stems. The older bark of the branches is a grayish-green color, and the younger stems are green, sometimes with a hint of pink. Mountain whitethorn has impressive and protective thorns that can, in some cases, protrude beyond the leaves and flowers, and accidentally leaning or sitting on it can be a painful experience. The small, elliptic, three-veined leaves are sage green and are darker in color on the surface and paler beneath. Some of the leaves may exhibit a small, notched indentation at the leaf tip.

Clusters of faintly fragrant, creamy white flowers adorn the branch ends. Once pollinated, the flower develops into a small, pronounced, three-lobed capsule, with each lobe having a crested valve. The fruit is a mixture of red and green hues, sometimes striped or spotted, making this shrub quite striking in late summer or early autumn when found in large groupings.

Mountain whitethorn favors dry, sunny, exposed to partially shady openings on slopes or ridges in mixed coniferous forests and woodlands. It is known to promote high-intensity wildfires and can easily sprout from the roots after being burned over. In many giant sequoia groves where prescribed fire is practiced, mountain whitethorn can grow rapidly in charred areas and provide initial habitat for wildlife.

BOTANICAL FAMILY: Rhamnaceae

ELEVATION: 3,000–9,500 ft (900–2,900 m)

DISTRIBUTION: Lower and upper montane, subalpine

HEIGHT: Up to 5 ft (1.5 m)

FLOWER, FRUIT, OR CONE: Clusters of small, aromatic, creamy white flowers on branch tips

HABITAT: Open, sunny ridges, mixed forests and woodlands, and chaparral

Sierran Gooseberry
Ribes roezlii

The grayish-brown branches of the deciduous Sierran gooseberry arch upward stiffly. On older stems, this shrub has stout, straight spines that are nearly hidden underneath the small, nodal, palmate leaves, and leaning or sitting on these sharp prickles will leave a lasting impression. The leaves occur in loose clusters arising from spiny nodes, and the beautiful, purplish-red flowers hang in pendulous clumps.

The showy, reddish-purple sepals are tightly reflexed, and the white petals hang straight down. Long, readily observed, greenish anthers protrude from the petals. The flowers are reminiscent of small, cultivated fuchsia flowers. When pollinated, the inferior ovary swells into a green, prickled fruit that matures into a bright red berry covered in defensive spines.

This nutritious edible berry is an important food source for many species of wildlife that inhabit the Sierra Nevada—species that, in turn, become important agents for spreading the seeds. Wildfires also encourage the growth and success of this native shrub, which can be found in dry to moist, open or shady forests, woodlands, and chaparral. Eradication efforts by the U.S. Forest Service and the Civilian Conservation Corps were pursued from the 1930s until the 1960s because the gooseberry functions as an intermediate host for the fungus that causes white pine blister rust, which can afflict stands of desirable sugar pine. It has since been learned that frequent, low-intensity fires mitigate the threat of blister rust.

BOTANICAL FAMILY: Grossulariaceae

ELEVATION: 3,400–8,500 ft (1,050–2,600 m)

DISTRIBUTION: Lower and upper montane, subalpine

HEIGHT: Up to 5 ft (1.5 m)

FLOWER, FRUIT, OR CONE: White petals encased in reflexed, reddish-purple sepals

HABITAT: Open or shady coniferous forests and woodlands

Thimbleberry

Rubus parviflorus

Thimbleberry is an ascending, deciduous, perennial shrub with woody, grayish-brown bark. New stems are bright green and topped with velvety-soft, green leaves, generally five-lobed with toothed margins, similar to the shape of maple leaves. Autumn brings a yellow, pale peach, or russet color to the lush leaves, creating a striking display when the shrub appears en masse in an evergreen forest.

The petioles and sepals are glandular and slightly hairy, and the sparse, terminal flowers are arranged in a cyme—an inflorescence in which the upper or central flower blooms prior to the lower flowers. Five white, oval to round petals surround numerous thin, yellow stamens. The superior ovary matures into a soft, sweet, red, aggregate fruit that, when plucked, separates easily from the receptacle as a thimble-shaped berry.

The shrub is generally located as small, knee-high patches in moist areas in shady to partially shady mixed coniferous forests and woodlands. Thimbleberry contrasts with other native berries in that it is completely devoid of prickles or thorns. Highly prized by wildlife and humans alike, the delicate, many-seeded berry can be eaten raw or dried, or made into jam.

BOTANICAL FAMILY: Rosaceae

ELEVATION: 3,600–8,200 ft (1,100–2,500 m)

DISTRIBUTION: Lower and upper montane, subalpine

HEIGHT: 2–7 ft (0.6–2 m), but sometimes reaching 8 ft (2.4 m)

FLOWER, FRUIT, OR CONE: White flowers with yellow stamens, maturing into red, aggregate fruits

HABITAT: Shady or partly open, moist mixed forests and woodlands

Whiteleaf Manzanita

Arctostaphylos viscida subsp. *mariposa*

Whiteleaf manzanita is a multibranched shrub recognized by its smooth, reddish-brown bark and dense, heavy wood. Manzanita bark is characteristically paper-thin and sometimes can be seen peeling back in small curls. The thinness of the bark allows for surface transpiration, so on hot summer days the bark may feel cool to the touch, due to water evaporating through the tissue. The shrub's sinuous and picturesque limbs may have areas of dead, gray tissue that appear as small, linear sections along branches or as entire deceased twigs. Colorful fruticose lichens can sometimes be seen growing on this dead wood. The round, flat leaves, which have smooth margins and pointed tips, are a pale, whitish sage green color. Compare these slightly fuzzy, pale leaves to the dark, smooth leaves of the greenleaf (see page 32).

The small, urn-shaped, pinkish-white flowers droop in panicles from hairy, glandular pedicels. When pollinated, the flower develops into a mature fruit that is sticky, small, round, and reddish brown, with a minute amount of dry flesh encasing many stone-like seeds. *Manzanita*, a Spanish word meaning "little apple," refers to this berrylike fruit, which is an integral part of the autumn diet for some species of Sierra Nevada wildlife.

Whiteleaf manzanita grows on dry, open, or rocky slopes in chaparral, oak woodlands, and sunny coniferous forests. It is a drought tolerant, versatile, and valuable shrub of warmer ecosystems in California.

BOTANICAL FAMILY: Ericaceae

ELEVATION: 500–6,100 ft (150–1,850 m)

DISTRIBUTION: Foothills, lower montane

HEIGHT: 3–10 ft (0.9–3 m)

FLOWER, FRUIT, OR CONE: Urn-shaped, white flowers, maturing into small, round, reddish-brown fruits

HABITAT: Exposed warm ridges and open mixed forests, woodlands, and chaparral

FLOWERS

Alpine Lily

Broad-Leaved Lupine

California Cone-Flower

California Corn Lily

Crimson Columbine

Hartweg's Iris

Lemmon's Wild Ginger

Pacific Bleeding Heart

Pinedrops

Rattlesnake-Plantain

Seep Monkeyflower

Sierran Dwarf Rose

Snow Plant

Spotted Coralroot

Stream Violet

Trail Plant

Washington Lily

Western Wallflower

White-Flowered
Bog-Orchid

White-Veined Wintergreen

Wood Strawberry

Alpine Lily

Lilium parvum

When wandering in the shady forests of the Sierra Nevada, you may be fortunate enough to come upon the striking alpine lily. Its lower, linear leaves radiate from and surround the slender green stems. Higher up, the single, smaller leaves subtend the stems of the flowers.

Many showy flowers are borne on the stalk, blooming from bottom to top, so the flowers may be at full bloom at the bottom but still in bud at the top. The recurved, bright orange calyx and corolla reveal scattered brownish spots, and the stamens and pistil are easily seen protruding from the flower. The calyx and corolla together are referred to as the "perianth." In the case of the alpine lily, the entire perianth is a reddish to orange color with showy spots, which makes for an unforgettable encounter in montane areas. If pollinated, the flower develops into a greenish-brown capsule.

The alpine lily is found in riparian areas, near seeps and springs, and in moist coniferous forests. Cultivated lily varieties, available from nurseries, are treasured by many gardeners as focal points in their gardens.

BOTANICAL FAMILY: Liliaceae

ELEVATION: 4,600-9,500 ft (1,400-2,900 m)

DISTRIBUTION: Lower and upper montane, subalpine

HEIGHT: Up to 5.5 ft (1.7 m)

FLOWER, FRUIT, OR CONE: Showy orange flowers with recurved petals and spots

HABITAT: Riparian areas, wet meadows, and damp forests

Broad-Leaved Lupine

Lupinus latifolius var. *columbianus*

The palmate leaves of the broad-leaved lupine are unmistakable. "Palmate" refers to numerous leaflets fanning out from a common point, similar to the fronds of a palm or the outspread fingers of a hand. The lupine's large leaves occur both basally and distributed along the green stems. The underside of the leaves is slightly paler than the upper side.

The racemes of blue and white flowers bloom successively from bottom to top in an indeterminate manner. The blossom is made up of a banner, wings, and a keel. The banner is the broad, upright petal that has an irregular patch of white near its base. The two lateral wing petals nearly cover the ciliated keel. After pollination, the many-seeded pods are pendulous and slightly hairy.

Broad-leaved lupines put on a spectacular show in the early summer months, especially when massed over large areas. These lupines are adaptable and can be found in damp or riparian areas of meadows or forests. The genus name *Lupinus* originates from the Latin name for wolf, *Canis lupus*. Lupines and other plants in the Fabaceae family were once mistakenly believed to leach nutrients from soil. But because they have root nodules that fix nitrogen, they actually enrich depleted soils.

BOTANICAL FAMILY: Fabaceae

ELEVATION: 3,000–11,500 ft (900–3,500 m)

DISTRIBUTION: Lower and upper montane, subalpine, alpine

HEIGHT: 1–8 ft (0.3–2.4 m)

FLOWER, FRUIT, OR CONE: Showy purplish-blue racemes of asymmetrical flowers

HABITAT: Riparian areas and moist, shady meadows, slopes, and forests

California Cone-Flower

Rudbeckia californica

The California cone-flower is one of the most striking large, bright-yellow flowers in the Sierra Nevada. On tall stems, the composite flowers are held above elliptic or lanceolate leaves with entire or toothed leaf margins. In general, the underside of the leaf is hairy and lighter in color than the upper side. Leaves lower on the stem are larger, with the upper leaves becoming smaller toward the apex.

The showy flower is made up of sterile, yellow ray flowers and fertile, chartreuse disk flowers. The tiny disk flowers crowd atop a cone-shaped receptacle that is surrounded radially by the yellow ray flowers. Fertilized, disk flowers mature into a scaled, brown pappus.

California cone-flower is most often found in riparian areas, seeps, springs, meadows, or moist forested areas. It sometimes shares habitat with other flowers in the Asteraceae family and may be initially confused with them. The tall cone of tiny disk flowers of this species set it apart from other native, yellow, sunflower-type blossoms, which instead reveal flat or dome-shaped centers.

BOTANICAL FAMILY: Asteraceae

ELEVATION: 5,400–8,500 ft (1,650–2,600 m)

DISTRIBUTION: Lower and upper montane, subalpine

HEIGHT: 2–6 ft (0.6 to 1.8 m)

FLOWER, FRUIT, OR CONE: Showy yellow ray florets and chartreuse disk florets

HABITAT: Meadows and moist mixed coniferous forests and woodlands

California Corn Lily
Veratrum californicum var. californicum

The tall, thick, hollow stems of the California corn lily are sheathed alternately by many large, oval, bright green leaves. The leaves exhibit a strongly veined pattern, nearly ribbed in some cases; they are also vaguely reminiscent of the leaves of domesticated corn, hence the common name. In autumn, the bold leaves turn shades of yellow, ochre, or tan.

In advantageous years, the inflorescence spreads upward into a dense panicle of flowers. The creamy white flowers have six petals, streaked with pale green, on hairy stems. The fruit is an oval capsule with winged seeds.

California corn lily inhabits riparian areas, seeps, springs, and moist meadows and forest areas. It is adaptable and can be found at many elevations. At lower elevations it can reach its largest heights, whereas in the upper reaches of its distribution it becomes more diminutive in size. This showy plant does not produce blossoms every year. The leaves are distinctive and can provide extensive coverage in wet meadows. The corn lily contains alkaloids that are toxic to wildlife and humans.

BOTANICAL FAMILY: Melanthiaceae

ELEVATION: 3,300–11,500 ft (1,000–3,500 m)

DISTRIBUTION: Lower and upper montane, subalpine, alpine

HEIGHT: 3–6 ft (0.9–1.8 m)

FLOWER, FRUIT, OR CONE: Tall panicles of creamy white flowers above large, oval leaves

HABITAT: Wet meadows and moist mixed forests and woodlands

Crimson Columbine

Aquilegia formosa

The crimson columbine is a very striking, interesting, and beautiful flower of the Sierra Nevada forest landscape. Most of the three-lobed, toothed leaves are found near the base of the plant, in an open and airy arrangement. Long, slender stems emerge from the basal leaves, holding the apical, pendulous flowers aloft, either solitary or in few-flowered racemes.

The showy flower is comprised of five lateral, petallike, red sepals that protrude alternately through the five true petals, which are yellow, transitioning to orange and red at the tips of the hollow spurs. Pollinators are attracted to the flaring, nectary spurs of flowers in the columbine genus. The fruit is a five-headed follicle that develops into a shape similar to a jaunty jester's hat. The fleshy, green follicles eventually mature into dry, pale brown, many-seeded fruits.

Crimson columbine is found in riparian areas, seeps, springs, wet meadows, and moist, shady forests and woodlands. The Latin word used for this genus, *Aquilegia*, refers to the flower's looking like an eagle's (*aquila*) talon. Be alert for pollinators visiting the columbine; it is a special sighting to view hummingbirds flying below the nodding flowers to access the nectar spurs.

BOTANICAL FAMILY: Ranunculaceae

ELEVATION: 3,000–10,800 ft (900–3,300 m)

DISTRIBUTION: Lower and upper montane, subalpine, alpine

HEIGHT: 8–31 in (20–79 cm)

FLOWER, FRUIT, OR CONE: Showy red and yellow flowers with spurs and exserted stamens

HABITAT: Riparian areas and moist mixed woodlands and meadows

Hartweg's Iris
Iris hartwegii

Strong, green stems and linear, flat, basal leaves subtend the showy, pastel flowers of the Hartweg's iris.

The flower parts can be found in hues of white, yellow, or violet. In most cases, the outer perianth petals are larger and partly ruffled at the edges, and have dark purple or lavender venation. The inner perianth petals are narrower, more lance shaped, and less prominently veined. At the center of the blossom, arched, petallike reproductive structures nearly hide the stamens and stigma. The fruit is a leathery, oblong capsule.

Hartweg's iris prefers shady mixed coniferous forests and woodlands, or dry, open slopes and ridges. This native iris usually grows solitary or in small, scattered groups and is slender enough to be easily overlooked. Cultivated members of the iris family grace many a household and formal garden. The wide array of bold monochromatic or contrasting colors, and interesting shapes, of iris cultivars make them a favorite among horticulturalists.

BOTANICAL FAMILY: Iridaceae

ELEVATION: 2,000–7,500 ft (600–2,300 m)

DISTRIBUTION: Lower and upper montane

HEIGHT: 4–16 in (10–41 cm)

FLOWER, FRUIT, OR CONE: Showy veined flower in white, yellow, or violet hues

HABITAT: Open or shady mixed coniferous forests and woodlands

Lemmon's Wild Ginger

Asarum lemmonii

Lemmon's wild ginger is a perennial that grows vertically from tuber-like rhizomes and spreads to form a ground cover. Its large, lush, heart-shaped leaves arise from the forest soil on green petioles and exhibit smooth margins. The leaves are deep green on top and paler green on the underside, with a network of veins that can give the surface a quilted appearance. They tend to be evergreen in most habitats but sometimes brown at the edges if subjected to severe winter temperatures. However, if covered with a significant layer of insulating snow, they can remain green, awaiting the springtime thaw.

The nearly hidden flower grows close to the ground and is overshadowed by the showy leaves. The leaves must be gently turned back to reveal the brown to purple, bell-shaped flower. Three sepals are fused into a tube near the bottom of the flower and, at the apex, they flare out and reflex backward to tapered points. The inconspicuous flowers are glabrous within and softly hairy on the outside. Upon close examination, red-tipped anthers can be seen in the throat of the flower. The fruit of the wild ginger is a fleshy, rounded capsule, sometimes with persistent, clinging remnants of the calyx.

This aromatically spicy ground cover grows in damp or wet, shady or partially shady coniferous forests. Nearly all botanical parts of this native species have a pleasant smell similar to cultivated ginger.

BOTANICAL FAMILY: Aristolochiaceae

ELEVATION: 3,600–6,200 ft (1,100–1,900 m)

DISTRIBUTION: Lower and upper montane

HEIGHT: 3.5–8 in (9–20 cm)

FLOWER, FRUIT, OR CONE: Inconspicuous, brownish-red flowers under large, glossy leaves

HABITAT: Shady, cool, moist areas in mixed coniferous forests

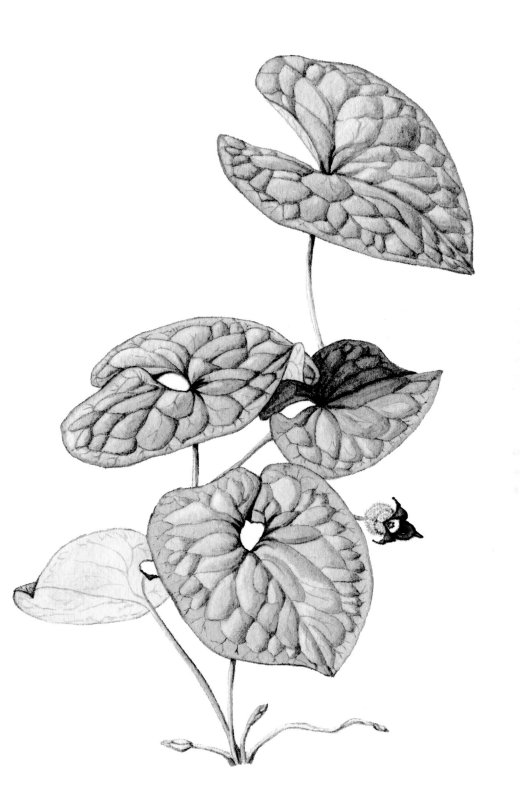

Pacific Bleeding Heart
Dicentra formosa

Pacific bleeding heart is a denizen of shady forests. Upon emergence, its finely dissected basal leaves sometimes have the appearance of a feathery fern.

Soon, curled heads of flowers begin to unfurl their beautiful, pouched, pink flowers above the foliage. Close inspection reveals that the nodding flowers comprise a classic panicle configuration, with lower flowers along the stem blooming prior to the terminal flowers. The pale pinkish-purple flowers are heart shaped and have rounded spurs, and the tips of the outer petals are flared. If the flower is pollinated, its pink petals wither and retract around the elongated, green fruit as it develops.

The delicate, drooping flowers and feathery foliage of this native woodland flower make it desirable for shady home gardens. Cultivated varieties of bleeding heart, larger in size and with more brightly colored blossoms, are prized plants in the gardens of many horticulturists.

BOTANICAL FAMILY: Papaveraceae
ELEVATION: 3,600–7,200 ft (1,100–2,200 m)
DISTRIBUTION: Lower and upper montane
HEIGHT: 8–18 in (20–46 cm)
FLOWER, FRUIT, OR CONE: Heart-shaped, pink flowers above feathery leaves
HABITAT: Riparian and damp areas, and shady forests and woodlands

Pinedrops

Pterospora andromedea

When strolling in the forests of the Sierra Nevada, one may encounter the tall, reddish-brown stems of pinedrops, a parasitic species that lacks chlorophyll and therefore depends on underground mycorrhizal fungi for nutrients (which the fungi derive from tree roots). Its inconspicuous, scalelike leaves occur at the very base of the stalk and can be nearly hidden in the woodland duff.

Its stem-like racemes are glandular, sticky to the touch, and composed of creamy to white, urn-shaped flowers with pedicels attached directly to the stem. The corolla is subtended by five reddish sepals that clasp the pendulous petals, which are united and have recurved tips. The flowers bloom successively from bottom to top, in an indeterminate manner. When mature, the fruit is a rounded, deeply cleaved and bisected, russet-colored, dry capsule.

The plant is found in open or shady mixed coniferous forests and woodlands. The new, pink racemes are conspicuous, emerging from the forest floor in late spring. Old, dry racemes can persist and remain an interesting feature for two years or even longer. Pinedrops, a much thinner and more camouflaged species, can be found in association with the much-celebrated snow plant. Pinedrops is an example of a North American monotypic genus, being the sole species of *Pterospora* found on this continent.

BOTANICAL FAMILY: Ericaceae

ELEVATION: 2,600–8,500 ft (800–2,600 m)

DISTRIBUTION: Lower and upper montane, subalpine

HEIGHT: 6–66 in (15–168 cm)

FLOWER, FRUIT, OR CONE: Small, pendulous, creamy white flowers on reddish-brown stalks

HABITAT: Open or shady mixed coniferous forests and woodlands

Rattlesnake-Plantain

Goodyera oblongifolia

Green stems of the rattlesnake-plantain rise out of a basal rosette of highly mottled and veined leaves. The cluster of leaves can be pale green to dark wintergreen, marked by highly variable, conspicuous, white veins. The basal leaves are perhaps the most striking feature of the rattlesnake-plantain and can entice people to take a closer look at its other interesting features. Its glandular and minutely hairy stems are sheathed with pale bracts.

The small, white flowers are primarily arranged along one side of the stem and are configured in a tight spiral near the top. The flowers are asymmetrical, comprised of two lower sepals that are spreading and flared, and an upper sepal fused to the upper lateral petals, forming a hairy hood over the other flower parts. The lower petal lip is like a pouch or sac and deeply grooved. If the flower is pollinated, the maturing fruit develops along the stem as a long, hairy capsule containing an abundance of tiny seeds.

The rattlesnake-plantain favors dry, partially to deeply shady mixed coniferous forests and woodlands. It is a species of orchid and prefers acidic soil and rich, decomposing forest duff with abundant leaf litter. Rattlesnake-plantain is sometimes confused with white-veined wintergreen, a dramatic plant that belongs to the heath family.

BOTANICAL FAMILY: Orchidaceae

ELEVATION: 1,600–7,200 ft (500–2,200 m)

DISTRIBUTION: Foothills, lower and upper montane

HEIGHT: 7–14 in (18–36 cm)

FLOWER, FRUIT, OR CONE: Hairy, beaked, white, irregular flowers in a raceme

HABITAT: Shady forests with needle or leaf litter and well-developed humus

Seep Monkeyflower

Mimulus guttatus

The green, ascending stems of the seep monkeyflower, an annual, can be smooth or slightly hairy. Its boldly veined leaves are oval to round, with profoundly toothed or dissected margins. The lower leaves have distinct petioles, and the upper leaves are sessile and clasped onto the stem.

A raceme adorns the apex of the seep monkeyflower with arresting flowers. The green, united calyx is cup shaped and prominently ridged, and the bright yellow corolla is asymmetrical, with upper and lower lips. The petals include a fused, two-lobed upper lip and a three-lobed bottom lip, in which the center lobe is distinctly larger than two lateral lobes. Typically, the lower lip is splotched with red and the inner, nearly closed throat is conspicuously hairy. The corolla drops off as the fruit develops into a five-ridged, indehiscent capsule.

This common, herbaceous flower is found nearly exclusively in wet habitats: riparian areas, seeps, springs, damp gravel, riverbanks, and moist forests and woodlands. Seep monkeyflower grows in many venues in the Sierra Nevada, from low to high elevations, as long as moist conditions exist. The Latin word used for this genus, *Mimulus*, translates to "comic actor" or "little mime," referring to the face-like appearance of the corolla.

BOTANICAL FAMILY: Phrymaceae

ELEVATION: 1,600–8,200 ft (500–2,500 m)

DISTRIBUTION: Foothills, lower and upper montane, subalpine

HEIGHT: 4–60 in (10–152 cm)

FLOWER, FRUIT, OR CONE: Asymmetrical, lipped, yellow flowers, sometimes with red spots

HABITAT: Riparian areas, isolated seeps, and springs in mixed forests or moist meadows

Sierran Dwarf Rose

Rosa bridgesii

Also called the Sierra ground rose or pygmy rose, this petite, native woodland rose has a mottled greenish stem with few prickles, generally paired, along the stem. The round leaflets have pronounced teeth on the margins and offer a good example of a pinnately compound leaf arrangement. The leaves are usually hairy and glandular, with tips that are truncate or blunt, not pointed.

The light to deep pink flowers, which have many yellow stamens at the center, are few to solitary and held aloft on glabrous stems. The mature fruit is red, fleshy, and round to ovoid, with green sepals persisting on the apex. The crimson-colored fruits of the rose family are often referred to as "rose hips" and are often rich in vitamin C. Because of this characteristic and their sweet carbohydrates, they are used to make tea, jam, jelly, syrup, wine, and other edible products.

The Sierran dwarf rose typically grows in dry, open to partially shady environments, such as mixed forests and woodlands, rocky ridges, and basins. This diminutive rose is sometimes seen in large groupings, almost as a ground cover, but more often as a solitary specimen. In either case, as a small woodland species growing beneath massive conifers, it offers an appealing contrast in size.

BOTANICAL FAMILY: Rosaceae
ELEVATION: 3,000–8,500 ft (900–2,600 m)
DISTRIBUTION: Lower and upper montane, subalpine
HEIGHT: 4–16 in (10–41 cm), but sometimes reaching 31 in (79 cm)
FLOWER, FRUIT, OR CONE: Small, saucer-shaped, pink flowers with numerous yellow stamens
HABITAT: Open or partly shady mixed forests, woodlands, and exposed ridges

Snow Plant

Sarcodes sanguinea

The fleshy snow plant provides an eagerly awaited Sierra Nevada botanical display. Typically making an appearance in late spring, this showy, red mycoparasite is a harbinger of the demise of winter. Mycoparasites are plants that draw on vast networks of soil fungi to transfer nutrients and water from coniferous roots to their own. When the snow plant emerges from the soil, it is bright red, with no green botanical parts.

A thick, stemlike raceme hosts red, linear, scalelike leaves that curve slightly over the bell-shaped flowers. The flower parts are assembled in groups of five: five sepals, five fused petals, and a five-chambered superior ovary. Deep within the urn-shaped flowers, and visible on close inspection, the pale white ovary is surrounded by ten yellowish-tan stamens that disperse their pollen from small, apical slits. The resulting fruit is a dry capsule encasing many tiny, brown seeds. Snow plant materializes from dry forest duff in open to shady mixed coniferous forests and woodlands.

This unusual species is monotypic in western North America, being the lone species of its genus *(Sarcodes)* in the region. Thomas Hill, a famous Western artist who had a studio adjacent to Yosemite's Wawona Hotel, chose the striking snow plant as a subject for one of his beautiful still-life oil paintings.

BOTANICAL FAMILY: Ericaceae
ELEVATION: 3,300–10,200 ft (1,000–3,100 m)
DISTRIBUTION: Lower and upper montane, subalpine, alpine
HEIGHT: 6–12 in (15–30 cm)
FLOWER, FRUIT, OR CONE: Bright-red stem, leaves, and bell-shaped flowers
HABITAT: Dry mixed coniferous forests with deep duff and well-developed humus

Spotted Coralroot

Corallorhiza maculata var. *maculata*

The genus name of this species, *Corallorhiza*, refers to its rhizome, an underground stem that grows roots and shoots. The thickened rhizome resembles the head of an aquatic coral. The upright stems are reddish to pale yellow with similarly colored, linear, sheathing leaves.

The openly spaced, indeterminate flowers are asymmetrical and sit atop a twisted, inferior ovary. It is a member of the orchid family and as such has flower parts in groups of threes, with three sepals that resemble petals. The veined, reddish sepals arch around two shorter pinkish, lateral petals. A lower, liplike petal is large and white, splotched with irregular, purplish spots of varying color intensity and size. The truncated, spotted dominate petal is generally crenate, having a scalloped edge. The exposed reproductive structures are columnar and, if pollinated, produce a drooping, red, faintly striped capsule.

Spotted coralroot grows on dry, open to shady, coniferous forest floors thick with decomposing needles. It is sometimes undetected due to its purplish-red coloration, which camouflages it amidst the leaf litter in shady or dark areas beneath the forest canopy. Spotted coralroot has a less common relative, striped coralroot, which is found in similar habitats. Instead of splotched petals, striped coralroot displays striped, reddish sepals and petals. One must get down on hands and knees to observe the subtle differences between these two orchids. The two coralroots, along with pinedrops (see page 66) and the snow plant (see page 74) are fascinating parasites on soil fungi. Because they take their food from underground, they do not need the green chlorophyll that their relatives use to make food from sunlight.

BOTANICAL FAMILY: Orchidaceae

ELEVATION: 3,900–9,200 ft (1,200–2,800 m)

DISTRIBUTION: Lower and upper montane, subalpine

HEIGHT: 7–22 in (18–56 cm)

FLOWER, FRUIT, OR CONE: Reddish sepals and some reddish petals, with prominent lower white petal exhibiting purple spots

HABITAT: Dry, shady coniferous forests with deep duff and humus

Stream Violet

Viola glabella

Bold, bright green, heart-shaped leaves with toothed margins may herald one's initial acquaintance with a stream violet. This perennial has large, basal leaves ascending to smaller, similar-shaped leaves near the top of the peduncle. One might encounter other yellow violets in sequoia groves (such as the wood violet with its deeply lobed leaves), but none have the wide, heart-shaped leaves of this species.

The yellow flowers are arranged in a loose cluster above the foliage. The bilaterally symmetrical, five-petal flowers have two upper banner-like petals without veins, and two lateral petals and a lower, spurred petal displaying minute, purple veins. The fruit of the violet is an oblong to oval-shaped capsule with minute appendages. Along with other violets, stream violet often has cleistogamous flowers dispersed among the other, showier blossoms or appearing after them. To observe them, look for smaller, inconspicuous flowers that may appear as closed buds. These closed, nonblooming, specialized cleistogamous flowers are self-pollinating. This extreme method ensures pollination, perhaps at a less favorable time of the flowering season. Cleistogamous flowers often produce more viable seeds than earlier-blooming, more pollinator-accessible flowers.

BOTANICAL FAMILY: Violaceae

ELEVATION: 3,300–8,500 ft (1,000–2,600 m)

DISTRIBUTION: Lower and upper montane, subalpine

HEIGHT: 1–15 in (2.5–38 cm)

FLOWER, FRUIT, OR CONE: Yellow, bilaterally symmetrical flowers, some petals with purple veins

HABITAT: Shady riparian areas, seeps, springs, and moist meadows

Trail Plant

Adenocaulon bicolor

Trail plant has distinctive, deltoid, mostly basal leaves. The large, veined leaves are borne on long petioles and have shallowly lobed margins. They are bright green on top and thickly tomentose (matted with dense, interwoven, woolly hairs) on the pale gray underside. Smaller leaves that mimic the appearance of the basal leaves are dispersed along the ascending stem.

Tiny panicles of white flowers are held aloft on slender stems. Upon close inspection, one sees that the corolla consists of an outer group of pistillate flowers and an inner group of staminate disk flowers. The mature fruit is green, lightly striped, and oblong to club shaped, and minuscule stalked glands are scattered over the fruit and along the upper stem.

The locale of trail plant is generally moist soils beneath a shady or partially shady canopy of forest and woodland trees. Trail plant may serve as a guide when walking and exploring in the forest. When hikers (or animals) brush against its bold, basal leaves and turn them over, their conspicuous, woolly, pale undersides provide a strong indication of the path recently taken. This characteristic of the overturned leaves, in fact, provides the origin of this plant's name.

BOTANICAL FAMILY: Asteraceae

ELEVATION: 3,000–6,600 ft (900–2,000 m)

DISTRIBUTION: Lower and upper montane

HEIGHT: 1–3 ft (0.3–0.9 m)

FLOWER, FRUIT, OR CONE: Inconspicuous white flowers amidst showy basal leaves

HABITAT: Riparian areas and shady, moist forests and woodlands

Washington Lily
Lilium washingtonianum

It is a spectacular and memorable experience to encounter a Washington lily in full bloom. Its tall, green stems arise from a rhizome-like bulb. Six to twelve whorled, oblong to lance-like leaves, with slightly wavy margins, radially surround the stem.

The large, intensely fragrant, white flowers bloom successively from bottom to top, in an indeterminate manner. Smaller leaflets subtend the stems of the blossoms. The flowers, which stand out from the stem horizontally to drooping, are flared or trumpet shaped. Tiny magenta to red spots freckle the interior of the perianth (the calyx and corolla collectively). The stamens are comprised of long, green filaments topped with creamy-colored anthers dusted with bright yellow pollen. Protruding from all of the other flower parts, the green pistil bears a three-lobed stigma at its tip. When the flower is pollinated, the fruit becomes an erect, cylinder-shaped capsule filled with many flat seeds.

Washington lily is found in sunny to partially shady mixed coniferous forest openings. This particular lily does not favor wet habitats, as most others do; rather, it thrives in open, forested areas that have been disturbed by roads, clear-cuts, or recent wildfires. Native lily species generally fail to flourish in home gardens; however, hybrid members of the lily family are avidly cultivated and prized plants in arboretums and botanical gardens.

BOTANICAL FAMILY: Liliaceae
ELEVATION: 1,300–7,200 ft (400–2,200 m)
DISTRIBUTION: Foothills, lower and upper montane
HEIGHT: Up to 8.5 ft (2.6 m)
FLOWER, FRUIT, OR CONE: Large, showy, white, fragrant flowers speckled with tiny spots
HABITAT: Open, partly shady, or recently burned areas in coniferous forests

Western Wallflower

Erysimum capitatum var. capitatum

The slender, perennial Western wallflower plant emerges from the mounded, dry, basal leaves of the previous year. The new, green leaves are oblong to lance shaped and usually have slightly toothed margins. The slim stems, which are generally solitary, are tall and easily spotted once the compact raceme of bright orange flowers begin to bloom.

A raceme is a configuration of unbranched flowers along a stem that bloom successively from the bottom toward the top, with each blossom supported by a small pedicel or stalk. Four round-ended petals, usually orange but more likely yellow as elevation increases, taper toward the center of the flower into a clawlike spur. The apical, clustered flowers are dense, with the lower, pollinated flowers elongating into a silique (a thin, elongated, many-seeded capsule-like fruit characteristic of the mustard family).

Western wallflower is a highly adaptable species, thriving in a variety of habitats. It can be found in dry, open to partially shady chaparral, woodlands, mixed coniferous forests, and rocky ridges, yet it can also flourish in disturbed soils or recently burned areas. Historical use of "wallflower" as a term for unpopular or shy individuals attending a party is a peculiar misnomer. Western wallflower is neither retiring nor subdued in color or appearance, and its delicate, sweet fragrance is exquisite—well worth kneeling close to bury one's nose in a single flower.

BOTANICAL FAMILY: Brassicaceae

ELEVATION: 1,600–8,200 ft (500–2,500 m)

DISTRIBUTION: Foothills, lower and upper montane, subalpine

HEIGHT: 8–31 in (20–79 cm)

FLOWER, FRUIT, OR CONE: Many orange, four-petaled flowers clustered at the apex of stems

HABITAT: Dry exposed ridges, slopes, and open mixed forests and woodlands

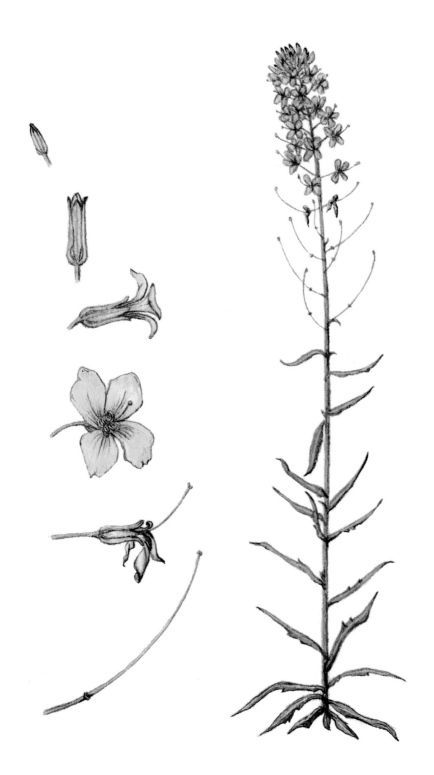

White-Flowered Bog-Orchid
Platanthera dilatata var. leucostachys

The tall, bright green stems of the white-flowered bog-orchid are sheathed with leaves that clasp near the base of the plant. Ascending along the stem, the clasping leaves decrease in size and become more linear in shape.

A tall spike of white flowers densely crowd around the stem. The upper sepal of the flower is partially fused with the upper petals in a hoodlike shape that arches over the reproductive structures. The lateral lower sepals are spreading and petallike. The upper petals are erect and nearly fused with the upper sepal. The lower petal is lip shaped and pendant, with a long, conspicuous spur curving downward behind the flower. The inferior ovary, if pollinated, matures into a capsule enclosing many minute seeds.

White-flowered bog-orchid is found in open, wet environments amidst mixed coniferous forests and woodlands. Be on the lookout for these beautiful orchids in bogs, marshes, seeps, springs, and riparian areas. Its small, intricate flowers are especially interesting for close observation, with or without the aid of a hand lens. Worldwide, orchids are an extremely large family, and many desirable species are prized for cultivation.

BOTANICAL FAMILY: Orchidaceae

ELEVATION: 3,900–11,100 ft (1,200–3,400 m)

DISTRIBUTION: Lower and upper montane, subalpine, alpine

HEIGHT: 6–60 in (15–152 cm)

FLOWER, FRUIT, OR CONE: Spike of small, white, asymmetrical flowers, each with a long spur

HABITAT: Riparian areas, moist meadows, marshes, seeps, and bogs

White-Veined Wintergreen
Pyrola picta

The aptly named white-veined wintergreen has conspicuous, pale, netted veins set against dark blue-green leaves. The basal, fleshy leaves vary in size and are oval to elliptic, with smooth margins. The pinkish stems rise from the cluster of leaves.

The small, pointed sepals are easily seen on the top of the flower because the open, bell-shaped flowers hang along the peduncle. White-veined wintergreen exhibits a classic indeterminate blossoming pattern, flowering successively from bottom to top. The five petals are white, sometimes tinted with green or pink hues. From the superior ovary, a single, long, exserted style protrudes distinctively beyond the petals and is tipped with a lobed stigma. When mature, the fruit is a pendulous, drooping, valved capsule.

White-veined wintergreen is usually found in dry, open or shady to partially shady mixed coniferous forests and montane habitats. It seems to prefer acidic soils covered with sparse needle and leaf litter. It is a member of Ericaceae, the heath family, which includes species found in the circumboreal northern hemisphere, and also in cool and mountainous areas around the globe. At first glance, white-veined wintergreen may be confused with rattlesnake-plantain, due to their similar habitat and showy, basal leaves. But upon close inspection, the flowers are entirely different, and they belong to wholly disparate botanical families.

BOTANICAL FAMILY: Ericaceae
ELEVATION: 1,300–9,000 ft (400–2,750 m)
DISTRIBUTION: Foothills, lower and upper montane, subalpine
HEIGHT: Up to 14 in (36 cm)
FLOWER, FRUIT, OR CONE: Nodding white flowers above white-veined basal leaves
HABITAT: Dry, open or shady mixed coniferous forests

Wood Strawberry

Fragaria vesca

Strawberries propagate by seeds, underground rhizomes, and stolons. The petioles of wood strawberry leaves are covered with small hairs and hold aloft a sessile set of three leaves that are elliptic to oval in shape, with markedly serrate margins. Sometimes the leaf edges are slightly tinted with a red hue. The leaves are sparsely hairy above and more abundantly hairy on the underside.

Wood strawberry flower parts occur in sets of five: five sepals subtending five petals. The white flowers, with numerous yellow stamens, are flat and open and are arranged in a branched inflorescence referred to as a "cyme," wherein the uppermost flower blooms prior to lower flowers. The pistils are numerous and develop from a receptacle, which forms a fleshy, red fruit. The pistils, which remain small and are scattered on the surface of the edible fruits, are called "achenes." The strawberry is one fruit that bears its seeds on the outside of a desirable, sweet fruit, enhancing the opportunity for foraging animals to spread the seeds after ingestion. In fact, the small, bright red, ripe berries can be difficult to find because they are usually consumed by wildlife immediately upon maturation.

Wood strawberries are versatile and found in many habitats, especially damp or moist, shady to partially shady woodlands and forests.

BOTANICAL FAMILY: Rosaceae

ELEVATION: 100–6,900 ft (30–2,100 m)

DISTRIBUTION: Lower Sonoran, foothills, lower and upper montane

HEIGHT: 1–6 in (2.5–15 cm)

FLOWER, FRUIT, OR CONE: White-petaled flowers with numerous yellow stamens and small, red berries

HABITAT: Partly to deeply shady mixed coniferous forests and woodlands

SPORE-BEARING PLANTS

....

Common Scouring Rush

Western Bracken Fern

Common Scouring Rush

Equisetum hyemale subsp. *affine*

The common scouring rush is a tall, slender perennial that can be found in vast stands that originate from underground rhizomes. The generally hollow stems are green, rigid, erect, and coarsely ribbed on the outside. The stems are banded horizontally with prominent, sheathed nodes, which are two-toned, having dark, toothed perimeter edges and lighter centers.

On fertile stems, the apex is crowned with a pointed oval cone covered with intricate scales that have a dark spot in the center. Reproduction occurs in two ways: by spreading rhizomes, and by tiny, round, green spores.

This ephemeral, water-loving native can be found in any area with sufficient underground or surface water. The common scouring rush can be quite invasive if introduced into horticultural gardens, backyards, or near water features, and it is difficult to successfully eradicate once established. The family and genus names, Equisetaceae and *Equisetum*, refer to the Latin for horse, as in *equestrian*, and are clearly related to the common name horsetail. Although many people incorrectly guess that these plants are related to bamboo (which is a kind of grass), Equisetaceae are remnants of an ancient group that is older than the age of dinosaurs. This plant is tough and fibrous, and when scrunched or wadded up, it is quite effective in scouring pots.

BOTANICAL FAMILY: Equisetaceae
ELEVATION: 1,600–8,200 ft (500–2,500 m)
DISTRIBUTION: Foothills, lower and upper montane, subalpine
HEIGHT: 2–7 ft (0.6–2.1 m)
FLOWER, FRUIT, OR CONE: Sporangia located in a small terminal cone
HABITAT: Riparian areas, seeps, springs, moist forests, and woodlands

Western Bracken Fern
Pteridium aquilinum var. *pubescens*

The bracken fern is a familiar terrestrial species that spreads by lengthy rhizomes. In late spring, the tightly curled fiddleheads of the bracken fern break through the soil. In under a week, the coiled fronds unfurl into bright green, triangular fronds that are upright and ascending. In autumn, the fronds turn a deep yellow, progressing to tan and eventually pale brown in winter. The blades of the frond are divided into a twice-pinnate structure.

Along the margin of the underside of the frond you may find sori. A sorus is a cluster of reproductive sporangia on a fertile blade. Sometimes a slightly rolled leaf margin can obscure the sori.

Bracken fern is highly adaptable and grows in a wide variety of habitats, from moist to dry. It is a common component in the understory in mixed coniferous forests of the Sierra Nevada. The long rhizomes have traditionally been collected, dried, and coiled for later use as a vital material in basket weaving, and they continue to be used in this way. When the rhizomes are subjected to iron (e.g., soaked with rusty nails), they take on a deep, nearly black color, allowing for vibrant contrasting design patterns in basketry.

BOTANICAL FAMILY: Dennstaedtiaceae
ELEVATION: 3,600–9,800 ft (1,100–3,000 m)
DISTRIBUTION: Lower and upper montane, subalpine
HEIGHT: 1–8 ft (0.3–2.4 m)
FLOWER, FRUIT, OR CONE: Sori arranged beneath the leaf along frond margins
HABITAT: Damp or dry areas beneath open or shady mixed forest canopy

Glossary of Terms

achene. Dry, one-seeded fruit.

aggregate. Fruit formed from several separate ovaries.

anther. Pollen end of the stamen.

apical. Situated at the apex, or uppermost point.

basal. Having leaves clustered near the ground.

bilateral. Mirror-image halves divisible only one way.

bole. Tree trunk.

boreal. Northern regions dominated by conifers.

bract. Small, scale or leaflike structure.

calyx. Collective term for sepals that subtend the petals.

capsule. Dry, many-seeded fruit.

catkin. Spike of unisexual flowers, usually drooping.

cauline. Having leaves borne on a stem.

ciliate. Having hairs along the edge.

circumboreal. Encompassing the boreal regions.

cleistogamous. Having self-pollinating budlike flowers that do not open.

corolla. Collective term for petals.

corymb. Flat-topped inflorescence.

crenate. Having scalloped margins on leaf or flower edges.

cyme. Branched inflorescence that blooms from top to bottom.

deltoid. Triangular.

dissected. Irregular and deeply cut, usually leaves.

drupe. Fleshy, unopening, berrylike fruit.

endemic. Restricted to a particular region.

entire. Having smooth margins.

exserted. Projecting beyond an enclosing organ.

filament. Stalk holding up the anther.

fruticose. Characterized by a shrubby, branched growth pattern, usually lichen.

glabrous. Having a smooth surface.

glaucous. Having a white or powdery appearance.

herbaceous. Characterized by plant tissue that is soft, not woody.

indehiscent. Remaining closed persistently.

indeterminate. Having flowers that bloom from bottom to top.

inflorescence. Cluster of flowers in its entirety.

involucre. Clustered group of bracts.

lobe. Large projection on the edge of a leaf or flower part.

marcescent. Withered but still attached to the plant.

monotypic. A taxonomic group, usually a genus, having just a single representative species.

montane. Region between the foothills and the subalpine zone.

mycoparasite. Parasitic fungus that uses other fungi to gain nutrition.

nectary. Botanical structure secreting nectar.

node. Position from which botanical structures arise.

ovary. Enlarged part of the pistil that contains ovules.

palmate. Having leaf parts that radiate from a central point.

palynology. Scientific study of pollen.

panicle. Branched flower that blooms from bottom to top.

pappus. Aggregate of structures atop an inferior ovary.

pedicel. Stalk holding up a flower or fruit.

peduncle. Stalk of inflorescence bearing flower or fruit.

pendant. Hanging, drooping, or reclined.

perianth. Corolla and calyx collectively.

petal. Individual member of the corolla.

petiole. Leaf stalk, attaching leaf to stem.

pinnate. Shaped like a feather.

pistil. Female reproductive structure of a flower.

pistillate. Having fertile pistils.

pubescent. Covered with fine, short hairs.

raceme. Unbranched stem of flowers that blooms from bottom to top.

receptacle. Structure to which flower parts attach.

recurved. Curved downward or backward.

reflexed. Curved backward.

rhizome. Elongated, horizontal, underground stem.

riparian. Along the side of a river or body of water.

scale. A thin membrane resembling the scale of a fish.

sepal. Individual member of the calyx.

septum. A thin partition that separates structures.

serrate. Having leaf margins with sharp teeth.

sessile. Without any supporting stalk.

silique. Elongated, narrow, many-seeded fruit.

sorus (sori). Distinct cluster of sporangia in ferns.

spike. Sessile flowers in an unbranched inflorescence.

sporangia. Spore-producing organ, common in ferns.

spur. A hollow sac or tubelike projection, usually containing nectar.

stamen. Male reproductive structure of a flower.

staminate. Having fertile stamens.

stigma. Female receptacle for pollen, generally sticky.

stolon. Elongated ground stem forming roots and shoots.

style. Thin stalk that connects the stigma and ovary.

subtend. To occur immediately below.

tomentose. Having dense, matted, interwoven hairs.

transpiration. The process of water vapor passing through a membrane or pore.

umbel. Many flower pedicels fanning out from a common point.

understory. Vegetation between the ground cover and forest canopy.

valve. One of the parts when a capsule splits.

venation. Pertaining to leaf veins.

Plant Key

FRUITS

Drupe   Capsule   Aggregate   Achene   Silique

FLOWERS

Nectary

Hypanthium

Indeterminate

Pappus

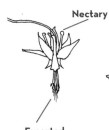

Exserted   Receptacle   Cyme   Corymb   Panicle

LEAVES   FERNS

Lobe

Venation

Bract

Node

Sporangia

Sorus (Sori)

Crenate   Dissected

SURFACES   GROUND STRUCTURES

Glabrous   Pubescent   Tomatose   Rhizome   Stolen

FLOWER PARTS

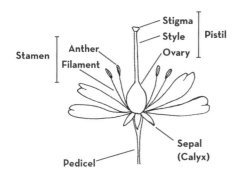

FLOWER ARRANGEMENTS

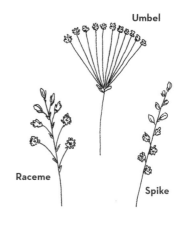

LEAF MARGINS

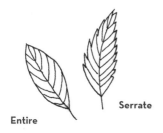

LEAF SHAPES

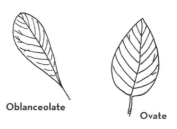

LEAF ARRANGEMENTS

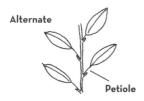

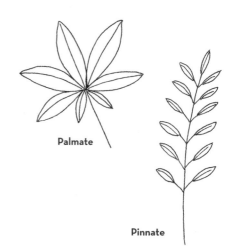

Acknowledgments

Appreciation to Belinda Lantz, Nicole Geiger, Jasmine Star, and the innovative, professional, and supportive staff of Yosemite Conservancy for making this book a reality. Thank you to Sierra Nevada experts Karen Amstutz, Pete Devine, Jeff Lahr, Jan van Wagtendonk, and Erik Westerlund for their professional input and feedback regarding the artwork composition and species selection.

Thank you to my dear friends Colleen Balch, Val Birkhoff, Todd and May Bristol, Bob and Sherry Engberg, Gayle Farmer, Glenda Gilreath, Ben Grodjesk, Giselle Hallam, Lou Lichti, Heidi Pusina, Heather Swan, Lori Weichenthal, and Becky Zentmyer for their encouragement and for continuing to remain engaged with what I was creating as I worked on this book for nearly three years.

Gratitude to my family members: Elizabeth Asunsolo, Kelvin Clark, Jen DesBois, Bill Haynes, Bryan Haynes, Liz Haynes, Robert Haynes, Jillian Lutes, Ted and Joyce Palaio, and Laura Wilkinson. You boosted my spirits with your positive comments and inexhaustible interest in the artwork.

Most of all, I must recognize the unlimited help, confidence, motivation, and insight given to me by my husband, Mark Spencer. Your ability to connect with my initial vision of this project and willingness to travel wholeheartedly with me on this creative journey are deeply valued and appreciated. Without your love and belief in me, the words and art that constitute this volume would never have been created. Thank you, Mark. I am most grateful to be sharing our lives together.

About the Artwork

I started taking art lessons during my childhood, and some of my earliest memories are of creating art that was appreciated and understood. Drawing and painting botanical renderings requires patience, accuracy, and a keen sense of seeing—really seeing. The intricate workings of the natural world regularly astonish and delight me: the fragile, yet tenacious, aspect of living things and how they function, grow, reproduce, and disperse. I am thankful for my science and art education, which enhances the experience of my life journey. That knowledge provides me with an understanding and appreciation of this stunningly beautiful world we inhabit. The pairing of art and science have shaped and defined me as a person, offering me an avenue to create beauty, foster understanding, and share my passion.

Many wonderful moments transpired in the nearly three years it took to create the watercolor artwork for this book. I spent many days sauntering in giant sequoia groves, observing and handling botanical specimens, taking photographs, and dreaming about pigments, techniques, and compositions. On brief winter days, I often painted with a purring kitty curled on my lap, with huge snowflakes drifting past the window, the wood stove crackling, and some of my favorite music playing in the background.

Exploring and savoring the beauty of a giant sequoia grove is one of my greatest pleasures in life. I feel fortunate to live adjacent to a vast grove, with its soaring canopy of green above enormous russet trunks sheltering an abundance of diverse and luxuriant life. Many of the botanical species in this book surround me as familiar and constant companions. It is a gift and privilege to stroll amongst the giant sequoias, and I am grateful for those who have valued these forests enough to nurture and protect them. I have long been inspired by the Sierra Nevada, particularly the unique habitats on the western slope. As artist and author, my hope is to imbue a sense of wonder and awe in you, awakening your own personal experience and relationship with nature.

References

Arno, S. F. 1973. *Discovering Sierra Trees*. El Portal, CA: Yosemite Association.

Blackwell, L. R. 1999. *Wildflowers of the Sierra Nevada and the Central Valley*. Renton, WA: Lone Pine Publishing.

Botti, S. J. 2001. *An Illustrated Flora of Yosemite National Park*. El Portal, CA: Yosemite Association.

Calflora Database. 2015. *Calflora: Information on California Plants for Education, Research, and Conservation*. http://www.calflora.org. Accessed from March 26 through April 28, 2015.

Gerstenberg, R. H. 1983. *Common Trees and Shrubs of the Southern Sierra Nevada*. Self-published.

Harrington, H. D. 1957. *How to Identify Plants*. Athens, OH: Swallow Press Books.

Hartesveldt, R. J., H. T. Harvey, H. S. Shellhammer, and R. E. Stecker. 2005. *The Giant Sequoia of the Sierra Nevada*. Honolulu, HI: University Press of the Pacific.

Hickman, J. C. 1993. *The Jepson Manual: Higher Plants of California*. Berkeley: University of California Press.

Hollender, W. 2010. *Botanical Drawing in Color*. New York: Watson-Guptill Publications.

Jepson Flora Project (eds.). 2015. *Jepson eFlora*. http://ucjeps.berkeley.edu/IJM .html. Accessed from March 26 through April 28, 2015.

Lanner, R. M. 1999. *Conifers of California*. Los Olivos, CA: Cachuma Press.

Laws, J. M. 2007. *The Laws Field Guide to the Sierra Nevada*. Berkeley, CA: Heyday Books.

Morgenson, D. C. 1975. *Yosemite Wildflower Trails*. El Portal, CA: Yosemite Association.

Pavlik, B. M., P. C. Muick, S. G. Johnson, and M. Popper. 2000. *Oaks of California*. Los Olivos, CA: Cachuma Press.

Spencer, S. 2009. *Flowering Shrubs of Yosemite and the Sierra Nevada*. El Portal, CA: Yosemite Association.

Storer, T. I., and R. L. Usinger. 1963. *Sierra Nevada Natural History*. Berkeley: University of California Press.

Stuart, J. D., and J. O. Sawyer. 2001. *Trees and Shrubs of California*. Berkeley: University of California Press.

Thomas, J. H. 1974. *Native Shrubs of the Sierra Nevada*. Berkeley: University of California Press.

West, K. 1983. *How to Draw Plants: The Techniques of Botanical Illustration*. New York: Watson-Guptill Publications.

Whitney, S. 1979. *A Sierra Club Naturalist's Guide to the Sierra Nevada*. San Francisco: Sierra Club Books.

Willard, D. 2000. *A Guide to the Sequoia Groves of California*. El Portal, CA: Yosemite Association.

Wilson, L., J. Wilson, and J. Nicholas. 1987. *Wildflowers of Yosemite*. El Portal, CA: Sierra Press.

Index of Common Names

Index of Scientific Names

About the Author

SHIRLEY SPENCER is a botanist, educator, and artist, specializing in Sierra Nevada natural and human history. She earned her B.A. in Life Science from Pacific Union College and M.A. in Environmental Studies from Fresno Pacific University. A gifted and versatile artist, Shirley specializes in watercolor; rendering botanically accurate illustrations as well as stylized portrayals of flora, fauna, and wilderness landscapes. Her field guide, *Flowering Shrubs of Yosemite and the Sierra Nevada,* featuring forty original watercolors, was co-published by Heyday and Yosemite Conservancy in 2009. In 2016, *Our National Parks Alphabet Book,* which Shirley wrote and illustrated, was published by Condor Designs. Shirley has worked in Yosemite National Park since 1979. She currently leads naturalist walks for Yosemite Conservancy, is a featured instructor for Road Scholar, and serves as a seasonal interpretive ranger for the National Park Service in Wawona. An avid mountain climber, trail runner, and cross-country skier, Shirley lives two miles from Yosemite's Mariposa Grove of Giant Sequoias with her husband, Mark.